COWGIRL UP

COWGIRL UP

Conceived and Written by Anna Chatterton

Co-created with Meg Braem and
Christine Brubaker

Cowgirl Up
first published 2023 by Scirocco Drama
An imprint of J. Gordon Shillingford Publishing Inc.

Scirocco Drama Editor: Glenda MacFarlane
Cover design by Doowah Design
Author photo by Benjamin Laird
Production photos by Benjamin Laird

Printed and bound in Canada on 100% post-consumer recycled paper.

Production inquiries to:
Ian Arnold Artist Representative, Catalyst TCM Inc.
www.catalysttcm.com

Library and Archives Canada Cataloguing in Publication

Title: Cowgirl up / conceived and written by Anna Chatterton ; co-created with Meg Braem & Christine Brubaker.
Names: Chatterton, Anna, author. | Braem, Meg, creator. |
Brubaker, Christine, creator.
Identifiers: Canadiana (print) 20230519377 | Canadiana (ebook) 20230519393 |
ISBN 9781990738272 (softcover) | ISBN 9781990738388 (epub)
Subjects: LCGFT: Drama.
Classification: LCC PS8605.H3925 C69 2023 | DDC C812/.6—dc23

We acknowledge the financial support of the Canada Council for the Arts, the Government of Canada, the Manitoba Arts Council, and the Manitoba Government for our publishing program.

J. Gordon Shillingford Publishing
P.O. Box 86, RPO Corydon Avenue, Winnipeg, MB Canada R3M 3S3

Dedicated to Frida,
my feisty cowgirl.

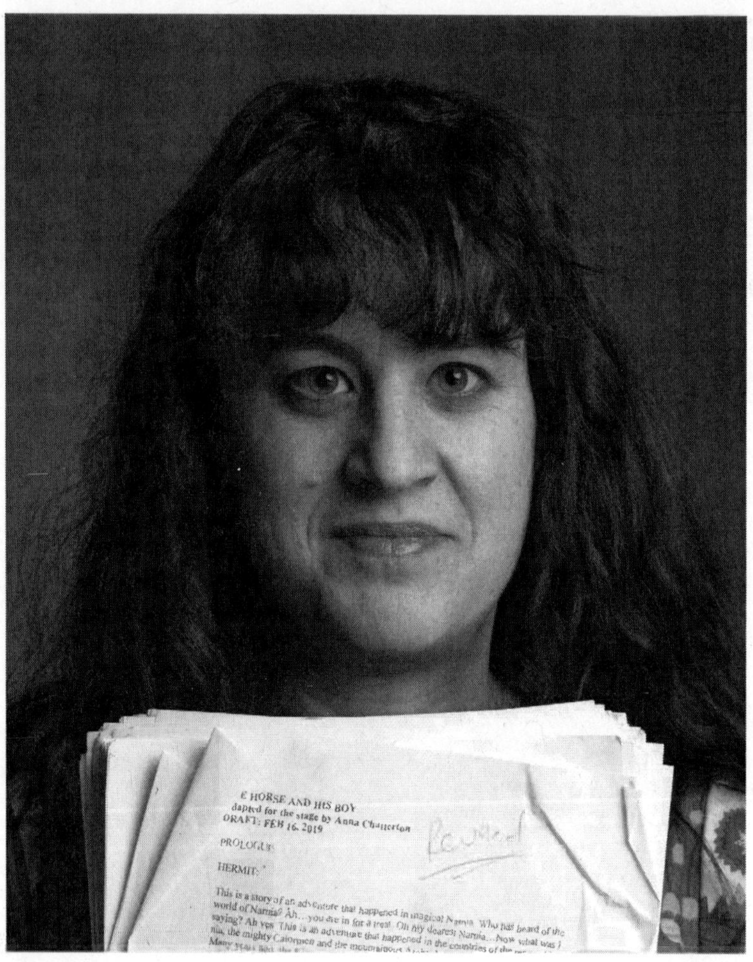
E HORSE AND HIS BOY
dapted for the stage by Anna Chatterton
DRAFT: FEB 16, 2019
PROLOGUE
HERMIT:

Anna Chatterton

Anna Chatterton is a librettist, playwright and performer based in Hamilton, Ontario. She is a two-time finalist for the Governor General's Literary Award for Drama for her plays *Gertrude and Alice* (cowritten with Evalyn Parry-Playwrights Canada Press), and *Within the Glass* (Scirocco Drama). Anna has been commissioned and produced by The Shaw Festival, Tarragon Theatre, Nightwood Theatre, Buddies in Bad Times, The Theatre Centre, Theatre Passe Muraille, and Canadian Opera Company, among others. As a librettist, Anna's work has been produced across Canada and the States and has been nominated for a Juno Award. She has been nominated for five Dora Mavor Moore Awards, winning Outstanding Production of an Opera, named a top ten Toronto Theatre Artist by Toronto's *NOW Magazine* and was a finalist for the 2019 Hamilton Literary Awards in Fiction for her play *Quiver*. Anna has been a playwright in residence at Tarragon Theatre, Nightwood Theatre, Tapestry Opera and at the National Theatre School of Canada. She teaches theatre courses at McMaster University, Humber College and Sheridan College.

Playwright's Note

It started with a postcard that was sent to me in black and white of a row of confident, happy cowgirls from the early 1900s. I was so struck by the joy on their faces, and the air of freedom they exuded, not typically seen in photos of women in those days. I loved the idea of the rhythm of horses and the lingo of rodeo. I also wanted to disrupt the iconic symbol of cowboys—putting cowgirls front and centre. And so, the idea of writing a play about cowgirls was born. Alberta Theatre Projects invited me out to Alberta to do some research and I went to an all-girls rodeo (hosted by The Canadian Girls Rodeo Association) where I interviewed cowgirls aged 14–85. I met barrel racer Skyler Mantler (who competed at the 2022 Calgary Stampede). Skyler and I talked on the phone one evening—me back home in Ontario on my couch, her riding her horse under the great prairie sky—and she told me stories about her Gran, Izzy Miller, one of the cowgirls who finally convinced the Calgary Stampede to showcase barrel racing in 1958 (thirty-plus years after other events at the big show). Skyler became a key inspiration for my protagonist Cassidy. I also met Effie Simpson, an infamous 83-year-old cussing cowgirl who I talked with on the phone frequently with pen in hand, ready to jot down her fantastic Effie-isms. Effie inspired the idea of the cowgirl goddesses and made it into the play—minus the cussing—in the form of her namesake, Goddess Effie. I had some long phone calls with two-time Canadian barrel racing champion Nancy Csabay who generously shared stories of when she was a young and ambitious barrel racer, and the story for *Cowgirl Up* materialized. I also steeped myself in years of deep research, learning the nitty-gritty of barrel racing, the huge job of caring for a horse, and rodeo culture. Then came the delicate dance of balancing fact with artistic licence to create a dramatic story.

A couple of years later, as dramaturge Meg Braem and director Christine Brubaker came on board, they began to offer ideas for the structure and story. This is typical with play creation, but it's rarely acknowledged in the theatre world, so we decided they should receive co-creation credits. I'd also like to acknowledge Eda Holmes and Andrea Donaldson for their crucial inspirations in the beginning stages of development, and Laurel Green for her belief in the play and helpful initial dramaturgy.

This is a love letter to all the resilient, hardworking cowgirls who do it for the love of it—remarkably similar to us artists.

Now, doncha ferget ta hoot an' holler when the announcer rallies you up!

Anna Chatterton

Acknowledgements

Other superheroes who helped get *Cowgirl Up* here—Joyce Lipsett, Dianne Goodman, Laura Mullin, Chris Tolley, Debbie Hambling, Kim Welter and a special thank you to the late Darcy Evans at ATP who originally programmed my play with the premiere slated for March 2020, but then, well, we all know the story.

Deep gratitude to all the talented actors who helped immensely along the way: Kiana Woo, Dylan Evans, Morgan Yamada, Elinor Holt, Sarah Wheeldon, Charlie Gould, Eric Wigston, Anna Cummer, Braden Griffiths, Ellen Close, Kira Bradley, Ayla Stevens, Helen Belay, Mike Tan, Trish Lindstrom, Kathryn Kerbes, Selina Wong, Makambe K. Simamba Courtney Ch'ang Lancaster, Mayko Nguyen, Dalal Badr, Jakob Ehman, Liz Saunders, Ericka Leobrera, Shayna Linds, Mykola Paskaru, Kit Simmons, Evalyn Parry and Megan Follows.

And of course, the stellar cast who premiered the play at ATP gave me such helpful thoughts and insight into their characters, the journey of the play, and colloquial language and phrasing—the play wouldn't be what it was without them.

And thank you to the ATP playwrights' units for your feedback: Louise Casemore, Adrienne Wong, Michaela Jeffery, Jan Derbyshire, David van Belle, Stephen Massicotte, Makambe K. Simamba, Cheryl Foggo, and Vern Thiessen.

And deep thanks to my family, who held up the fort while I made all the trips back to Alberta—our feisty Frida, Jim Ruxton and my mom Liz Chatterton.

Production Notes

Cowgirl Up is currently written for Alberta. If the play were produced in another province, it would be a simple change to make Cassidy from that province, and in Scene 5, she would be goin' down the road in rodeos from that province (with names of small towns and cities from that province), as there are rodeos in many provinces in Canada.

While the play is currently divided into two acts, if preferred, it could easily be performed as one act, with no changes.

Glossary

Buckle Bunny: female groupie of rodeo cowboys

Bulldogger: a steer wrestler

Cab: cabaret, rodeo dance

Farrier: a specialist in equine hoof care

Gymkhana: a day event for horse competitions

Over and under: a whip used to make a horse go faster

Pocket: the area around the barrel where the rider and horse will make the fastest turn

Rate: slowing the horse down before turning at the barrel

Starfish: putting both legs/stirrups straight out when riding

Timie: A cowboy that competes in a timed event (pronounced Time-ee)

Foreword

I remember the first time I was given directions to the Alberta acreage where my husband grew up… "You wanna pass the gas station on the left, you'll see Herman's ranch on the right, turn left at the green barn but if the road bends and you see the red barn, you've gone too far. Turn right on the gravel road at the other green barn (it's debatable whether it was green or blue) and you're there. You can't miss it."

I did. I missed it many times.

Turns out that ten years later, there was still a lot I was missing about Alberta.

By 2017, I'd been to the Calgary Stampede but only the midway. It was thanks to Anna Chatterton that I went to my first real rodeo. I met director Christine Brubaker, her daughter Ruby, and the gang from Alberta Theatre Projects on a cold morning at the Okotoks Agriplex. Anna was stuck in Toronto and would arrive the next day to begin a two-week workshop of her play. I remember the lights and the smell of hay and horses as we walked into the arena. I remember watching women casually chatting before they guided their horses away to get ready. We found our place in the stands and got ready to watch the competition.

Pound, pound, streak, heat, flash, fly!

Barrel racing is fast. Very fast. The barrel racers were so far ahead of me that my eyes could barely keep up. For the uninitiated, it can look like just a girl and her horse, but within those seconds, there is the bond between horse and human, the deft skill it takes to get a thousand-pound animal to melt around barrels, and the determination needed to sprint to the finish line. I tried to absorb what had just happened. The crowd was already cheering wildly.

As we watched, our eyes glued to ponytails flying under cowgirl hats, Effie strode up with her belt buckle shining. She stood triumphantly, cheering on each cowgirl. This was her world, and this new generation of barrel racers, her legacy. I finally realized that it is just a girl and her horse, that's all...and that's everything.

This play is a celebration of cowgirls everywhere. It's a celebration of rodeo life and of women supporting each other through adversity.

Without Anna Chatterton's bond to the rodeo community, the authenticity of this story wouldn't ring true. Without Christine Brubaker's deft direction, the audience wouldn't have felt the wind coming off the races. Without Alberta Theatre Projects' determination, this Alberta story would have gone untold.

Working on this play made me see Alberta differently. For the first time, I looked out as I drove up to the acreage where my husband grew up and saw the beauty of the big sky, the joy of horses running in the fields and the love people have for this way of life. It had been there all along, how could I have missed it?

It's been sixteen years since I moved to Alberta. It's my turn to invite people out to the acreage, letting them know, "You wanna pass the gas station on the left, you'll see what used to be Herman's ranch on the right, turn left at the green barn but if the road bends and you see the red barn, you've gone too far. Turn right on the gravel road at the other green barn (it's quite weathered now, so I'd call it grey rather than green) and you're there. You can't miss it."

Meg Braem
Spring, 2023

Meg Braem is an Alberta-based playwright and dramaturg. Her plays have been nominated for a Governor General's Literary Award and won the Alberta Literary Award for Drama, the Alberta Playwriting Competition and Playwright Theatre Centre's "The News Competition."

Production History

Cowgirl Up premiered October 20th, 2022 at Alberta Theatre Projects, Calgary, with the following cast and creative team:

Cast

Cassidy: .... Cara Rebecca
Starbright/Muffin: .... Darcy Gerhart
Effie: .... Karen Johnson-Diamond
Joyce: .... Katelyn Morishita
BB .... Rebbekah Ogden
Jed/Announcer/ Rebel/Lou: .... Richard Lee Hsi

Creative Team

Playwright:... Anna Chatterton
Direction by .... Christine Brubaker
Dramaturgy by .... Meg Braem
Choreography by .... Tania Alvarado
Assistant Direction by .... Camyrn Hathaway
Dance Captain: .... Richard Lee Hsi
Set and Lighting Design by .... Narda Mccarroll
Costume Design by .... Cathleen Sbrizzi
Sound Design by .... Peter Moller
Stage Management by .... Sara Turner
Assistant Stage Management by ..... Chandler Ontkean

Cassidy (Cara Rebecca) and Starbright (Darcy Gerhart) competing, Goddesses (Karen Johnson-Diamond, Katelyn Morishita, Rebbekah Ogden) cheering them on. Photo by Benjamin Laird.

Cassidy (Cara Rebecca) and Starbright (Darcy Gerhart) with Goddesses (Karen Johnson-Diamond, Rebbekah Ogden, Katelyn Morishita) goin' down the road. Photo by Benjamin Laird.

Cassidy (Cara Rebecca) and Starbright (Darcy Gerhart) with Goddesses (Karen Johnson-Diamond, Rebekkah Ogden, Katelyn Morishita). Photo by Benjamin Laird.

Starbright (Darcy Gerhart) waiting alone for Cassidy. Photo by Benjamin Laird.

Characters

CASSIDY: .... Twenties, barrel racer. Loner, determined, got fire in her.

JED: .... Late twenties. Professional tie down roper ("Timie" cowboy—his sport has a time). Pretty boy, tight pants, clean and pressed.

Cowgirl Goddesses:

EFFIE: .... Seventies, crusty, no-nonsense.

JOYCE: .... Late forties, 1980s power-cowgirl.

BB: .... Late twenties, intuitive, psychic.

STARBRIGHT: .... CASSIDY's horse, female. Speaks with horse inflections, lots of breath, is a bit beat poet-esque in how she talks too.

Also plays: MUFFIN.

ANNOUNCER/
REBEL/LOU .... played by actor playing JED

Setting

Mt Olympus Skybox, Canadian Rodeo Championships (CRC), Cabaret (rodeo bar)

ACT ONE

Scene 1

CASSIDY and STARBRIGHT doing a barrel race.

JOYCE: Heart beating fast, the thrill.

EFFIE: Rush of the wind, the speed.

BB: Feeling every muscle of your horse, the heat.

CASSIDY: And go and go.

STARBRIGHT: Raaace raaaace.

CASSIDY: Pace pace.

STARBRIGHT: Push whush.

CASSIDY: Burn turn.

STARBRIGHT: Pound pound.

EFFIE: Turning barrels makes time stand still.

BB: Horse warm under my thighs.

CASSIDY: Smooth.

STARBRIGHT: Smooth.

CASSIDY: Slick.

STARBRIGHT: Triiiick.

CASSIDY: Flow.

STARBRIGHT: Breeeeze.

CASSIDY: Squeeze.

STARBRIGHT: Huuug.

JOYCE: Crowds cheering just for you.

CASSIDY: Rock.

STARBRIGHT: Rolllll.

CASSIDY: Wrap.

STARBRIGHT: Coil.

EFFIE: Going fast as you can on a thousand-pound animal—

BB: With all the trust in the world—

JOYCE: Turning cans in the arena and running for home…

CASS/STAR: Pound pound streak heat flash fly!

Scene 2

High up Mount Olympus skybox.

EFFIE and JOYCE sit watching a large screen. They are wearing cowgirl hats. BB stands behind them, wearing a helmet.

ANNOUNCER V/O: Before we get to the Ladies' Barrel Racing, we'll take a moment to commemorate the history of Canadian Rodeo. Our forefathers—

EFFIE: Forefathers!

ANNOUNCER V/O: —are the world's best rodeo cowboys—Hank Abbie, Buddy Roy, Wayne Pederson, Monty Murray—all dirty, rotten, tough, cowboys.

EFFIE: Oh fer pete's sake. All ya see are cowboys for days.

JOYCE: And not one mention of any of us.

BB: Or Scamper. She oughtta be commemorated too.

EFFIE: They act as if cowgirls cracked outta stork eggs and landed riding barrel in the world's biggest outdoor rodeo. We started training at Tiny Mites Rodeos, Little Britches Rodeos, High School Rodeos. We fought long and hard to go pro.

JOYCE: And now we're just twiddling our goddess thumbs. What good is being a goddess if no one worships you? I'll tell you what gets me steamed.

EFFIE: Please don't.

JOYCE: I brought sparkle to the sport, I shone like the sun, I showed the world that cowgirls could be flashy and fierce competition. Now all you see is them Plain Janes in the saddle.

EFFIE: Less sparkle more dirt, so's you can be taken serious, not all decked out like a buckle bunny.

JOYCE: Nothing wrong with painting your nails red to cover the dirt underneath. Those girls are on the world stage. Where's the sparkle? Where's the glamour? It's like them girls are trying to fade into the background.

BB: Some of them didn't even make their own horses. Bought them trained to be pro. How can you know yer horse if you didn't watch 'em drop to the ground as foals?

EFFIE: We paved the way for all them fancy barrel racers and you think they know our names? Don't they know we just about had to beg to get barrel racing into the biggest rodeo? Now they're walking off with the biggest purse.

JOYCE: Thanks to me.

ANNOUNCER V/O: And first up is Lindsay Love from Okotoks on her fine horse Thunder…This little lady…

BB: Look at that gorgeous solid paint. I miss Scamper.

EFFIE: Dagnabbit. What I would give to be in the arena.

JOYCE: What I would give to have all them eyes on me.

BB: What I would give to have my own horse again. No one told me there would be no horses up here.

EFFIE: No one told me there would be no rodeo up here.

JOYCE: No one told me there would be no cowboys here, what kind of afterlife is that?

ANNOUNCER V/O: And they're off…nice and smooth now, okay, little wide around the…

EFFIE: Did you see that?

JOYCE: Almost had to look away.

EFFIE: She's flopping all over the place. She and the horse should be stuck together like Siamese twins.

BB: You mean conjoined twins. It isn't right to say Siamese.

EFFIE: Stuck together like I'm stuck with you two idiots. Can't shake ya no matter how hard I try.

JOYCE: Where's the sense of showmanship?

EFFIE: It isn't Vegas, Joyce. Rodeo is about two things: a cowgirl and her horse. Plain and simple.

BB: Horses are the ones shining.

EFFIE: A cowgirl's boots are just as dusty as a cowboy's, her eyes are just as sharp, but it's all about the bronc riding, the steer wrestling—man battling against the wild. Meanwhile we were doing it all and better, but we had ta battle to even get in the arena. And now, look at us, Joyce. Just look at us. Like it never happened.

JOYCE: Like we never happened.

BB: Are we just gonna sit here and complain for eternity?

EFFIE: What else you supposed to do once yer dead and passed over?

JOYCE: Besides look pretty as an angel.

EFFIE: Yer an old fart just like me.

JOYCE: Don't you lump me with you, Effie. Some of us have kept up our appearances. Not that there's anyone to notice.

BB: So get 'em to remember who you are!

EFFIE: What'er we supposed to do? Holler down at 'em? Hey humans! How's about you name a buckle after me? The Effie Simpson for All-Round Cowgirl!

JOYCE: Doncha forget Joyce Lipsett, the prettiest barrel racer that ever lived!

Beat.

EFFIE: Nothin. Them humans are dumber than a sack of hammers.

BB: So then put your money where your mouth is, cowgirls.

JOYCE: Whatcha mean?

BB: I'm talking about not just talking about it—

EFFIE: What the heck ya sayin?

BB: Don't talk, just do. Find a promising cowgirl and show her—

EFFIE: My tricks?

JOYCE: My treats?

BB: Show her how to be a champion.

EFFIE: You mean…go down to earth?

JOYCE: Can we really do that? Just leave the skybox?

BB: To save our legacy? Make sure we are remembered? You bet yer boots.

JOYCE: Do we get to come back?

BB: Once we done what we set out to do.

EFFIE: Alrighty then. No sweat. Give me one season and my cowgirl will be heading straight to the Canadian Rodeo Championships.

JOYCE: Give me one season and my cowgirl will be known to the world.

EFFIE: I'll bet my 24-karat gold plate buckle yer cowgirl will be crying 'cause she spent all her time thinking about her nails.

JOYCE: Yer 24-karat gold plate National Finals buckle?

EFFIE: You always wanted it.

JOYCE: Shoulda been mine to begin with.

EFFIE: It'll be mine till the end of time.

JOYCE: I'll be strutting the clouds with that buckle on my shiniest belt.

EFFIE: Yer on.

Scene 3

STARBRIGHT and CASSIDY at the Medicine Hat rodeo, in the alley waiting to compete.

ANNOUNCER: Alright, Medicine Hat, for all you new to the very fine event of Ladies' Barrel Racing, here's whatcha need to know. The cowgirls come in, turn a figure eight around the near side barrels, head down to the far side, complete that cloverleaf pattern with a third turn, and pull out all the stops in a lightning-fast run for home.

CASSIDY: Everyone's got someone in them stands but us.

STARBRIGHT: Uh huh uh huh.

ANNOUNCER: Now, of course we do have the penalty that can be incurred in a barrel race, that in the form of a knock-down barrel adding five seconds to the time. And you don't want to do that. The faster you go, the better you do. We time them electronically to one one-thousandth of a second.

CASSIDY: Gran should be here with us.

STARBRIGHT: Huh huh wuh wuh.

ANNOUNCER: First up is the beautiful lady Lisa Locklear from Dakota.

CASSIDY: Lisa Locklear, what's she doing in Medicine Hat? Aw, why does she have to be before me?

STARBRIGHT: Ruff ruff.

ANNOUNCER: This four-time champion is well known in these parts, won Calgary last year, number two rank cowgirl in the world, she won more money than anybody on her great horse Lucky, and she's back for a little more. Alright, girls, you know what to do, help help help her.

GODDESSES arrive in the stands.

EFFIE: Thunder and tarnation, it's good to be back.

JOYCE: Dazzling crowds.

BB: Look at all them horses! Buckskins, Quarters, Paints, Arabs, Appaloosas…

JOYCE: Look at 'em cowboys hangin on the gate.

ANNOUNCER: And she's off! Yes yes, perfect turns for Locklear and Lucky. How 'bout that for a cowgirl. Whooo, 14 point 798. What a ride. The best of the best. We'll see this cowgirl two-stepping at the cab tonight.

EFFIE: Wowee. That was one clean ride.

BB: Her horse sure did it for her.

JOYCE: Cowgirl had a snazzy shirt too.

EFFIE: Dagnabbit, been too long.

BB: The air is charged, and the animals are humming.

JOYCE: You know what's charging me is them tasty crop of cowboys…

EFFIE: I've met billy goats less horny than you, Joyce.

BB: Lisa Locklear looks like she's got it in the bag…one of you gonna choose her?

EFFIE: Too easy.

JOYCE: Already cooked.

EFFIE: Give me the underdog.

JOYCE: Give me the rookie.

EFFIE: They pay their entry fee just like everyone else. Give 'em to me and I can whip the last on the list and get her to first.

JOYCE: Oh, I can take the dowdiest gal and turn out a pageant queen.

BB: We were all nobodies once.

ANNOUNCER: And up next is Cassidy Clarkson, new around these parts with her pretty horse Starbright. Let's see how she do.

STARBRIGHT starts to buck.

STARBRIGHT: Ouuuuut. Ouuuuut. Tooooo Ji-tter twi-tter ruuuush fuuuuussss.

CASSIDY: /Hey, hey Starbright hey.

STARBRIGHT bucks more.

STARBRIGHT: Noooo nooooo tooooo boooom baaaammm. Ski-tter fri-tter.

CASSIDY tries to calm STARBRIGHT down.

ANNOUNCER: Just a moment now…seems to be some kind of holdup…

BB: Oh no, look, her horse is twitching.

EFFIE: Cowgirl looks too tense, no wonder her horse is acting up.

JOYCE: She looks like she wants to run away.

CASSIDY: C'mon Starbright, flee fly. Please. We can do this…Right?

STARBRIGHT: Riiiiight.

CASSIDY: Alright.

ANNOUNCER: Okey-doke, they're ready to roll. Running a little horse she calls Starbright, and the cowgirl on top is Cassidy Clarkson from Claresholm, Alberta. She comes here as a rookie, but she's come to town prepared to do battle on her buckskin.

CASSIDY and STARBRIGHT start to race.

CASSIDY: And go and go.

STARBRIGHT: Raaace raaaace.

CASSIDY: Pace pace.

ANNOUNCER: First barrel.

CASSIDY: Squeeeeze.

STARBRIGHT: Huuuuuug.

ANNOUNCER: Little too wide round the pocket.

EFFIE: Go go go!

ANNOUNCER: Alright now two turns to the right…

CASSIDY: Smooth.

STARBRIGHT: Smooth.

CASSIDY: Slick.

STARBRIGHT: Triiiick.

EFFIE: See the pocket. The pocket!

JOYCE: C'mon now!

ANNOUNCER: She's got it goin' on, okay, let's make one final turn. Third barrel.

JOYCE: Turn and burn…

CASSIDY: Wrap.

STARBRIGHT: Coooil.

They turn and knock the third barrel down.

ALL: Nooooooo.

ANNOUNCER: Oh no, she bumped it.

CASS/STAR: Pound pound.

CASS/STAR: Streak heat flash fly!

ANNOUNCER: With a barrel down that's gonna cost her five. Don't knock 'em down, you can knock 'em all around, just don't knock 'em down. 28.3. Keep your chin up, Cassidy.

The GODDESSES in the stands.

BB: Beaut of a horse.

EFFIE: She hasn't learned to get her horse on the right lead. Cued at the wrong time. But she's got good hands, I'll give 'er that.

JOYCE: Good-looking, too.

EFFIE: Good grief, looks can't help her win.

JOYCE: Her looks could make her a star, like yours truly.

EFFIE: I'd pick her up and get her back on her feet in no time.

BB: I'd make friends with her horse.

JOYCE: I'd teach her all my secrets to stardom.

EFFIE: I'd get her turning 'round those barrels Effie-style.

JOYCE: I'd make her a star, and hear them crowds roar.

EFFIE: That's my cowgirl.

JOYCE: That's my cowgirl.

BB: Yer both gonna choose the same girl?

JOYCE: Best of the worst.

EFFIE: Worst of the best.

BB: How's that gonna work?

EFFIE: *(To BB.)* You judge which goddess gets her there.

BB: Me?

EFFIE/JOYCE: You.

BB: O-kay.

JOYCE: *(To EFFIE.)* You in?

EFFIE You in?

EFFIE and JOYCE shake hands.

BB: We're on!

CASSIDY and STARBRIGHT in the alley.

CASSIDY: 28.3. Bottom of the list. We must have looked so stupid. Blast that third barrel.

STARBRIGHT: Waaaail waaaail.

CASSIDY: Wail wail, Starry. What the heck were we thinking that we could do this without Gran? I don't belong here.

CASSIDY turns and runs into EFFIE who has appeared behind her.

EFFIE: Hey, yer that cowgirl that just went on.

CASSIDY: Yeah, terrible ride.

JOYCE: Yer first time at Medicine Hat?

CASSIDY: Is it that obvious?

BB: *(To STARBRIGHT.)* Hey hey, pretty girl.

STARBRIGHT: Haaaaay huh huh haaaaay.

CASSIDY: Never seen Starbright so twitchy before.

STARBRIGHT: Heeeey, twiiitching, stiiiitching.

CASSIDY: Yeah, I was too.

BB: *(To STARBRIGHT.)* …such a sweet girl.

STARBRIGHT: Awwwwwe yeaaah yeeaah.

BB: What's her bloodline?

CASSIDY: Streaking Six.

EFFIE: Superior line.

BB: One of the best.

JOYCE: Sure is pretty. Both of ya.

CASSIDY: Uh, thanks. Made Starry myself.

BB: Good on you.

CASSIDY: Only way.

EFFIE: Got that right.

BB: *(To STARBRIGHT.)* See them cows?

STARBRIGHT: Yeah yeah mooooo yeah.

BB: Swish swish.

STARBRIGHT: Swish swish..

BB: Whisk whisk.

STARBRIGHT: Whisk whisk.

BB: Yeah, you can do better at the next one, right?

STARBRIGHT: Yeeeeah.

EFFIE: Keep off her head while you turn and you could make a lotta money.

JOYCE: Smile pretty and you'll charm the crowd.

CASSIDY: Wish I met you before I went in.

EFFIE: Now that you got this first race under yer belt, yer jitters will quit.

CASSIDY: That was our first and last race.

BB: What?

CASSIDY: We're heading home.

BB: You just got started.

CASSIDY: We made fools of ourselves.

JOYCE: Not winning doesn't mean you're a loser.

EFFIE: In my day we were just grateful to get in the arena. You don't turn down any opportunity to ride barrel.

JOYCE: Don't turn down any opportunity to be seen.

BB: Ever thought of goin' down the road?

CASSIDY: I don't have that kind of money.

EFFIE: Hogwash. Make money at the next one and you'll be on yer way to the CRC.

CASSIDY: Me?

EFFIE: Who taught ya to ride?

CASSIDY: My Gran...She passed last year. We were going to do this together.

BB: You don't have anyone here with you?

CASSIDY: No.

Beat.

EFFIE: Well, if ya listen to me, I can make ya slick, smooth, help ya melt round those barrels, get home faster than the rest.

JOYCE: Listen to me and people will be chanting your name in the stands.

CASSIDY: You all coaches?

BB: Actually, we're—

EFFIE makes sound to cut BB off.

JOYCE: Something like that.

BB: Effie here got barrel racing into the world's biggest outdoor rodeo. If it weren't for her, none of us cowgirls would be here.

CASSIDY: You did?

EFFIE: Darn straight I did.

BB: You'll find her in the Rodeo Hall of Fame.

JOYCE: Ahem.

BB: And you can thank Joyce here for getting the purse equal to the men's events.

CASSIDY: That's…amazing.

JOYCE: It sure was. I won Rodeo Queen and Best Cowgirl of the Year, same year.

CASSIDY: How did I not know that?

EFFIE: Bingo.

CASSIDY: When was that?

JOYCE: Oh, some time ago… BB's horse, Scamper, was inducted into the Pro Rodeo Hall of Fame

EFFIE: And was chosen The Horse with the Most Heart six years.

BB: Champion horse whisperer, at your service.

CASSIDY: Wow. Where did you say you were from?

EFFIE: Up.

JOYCE: North.

CASSIDY: Oh yeah? How far?

BB: Far as you can get.

CASSIDY: Like Fort Mac, or the Territories?

JOYCE: Oh, never mind us, much more exciting to talk about you.

CASSIDY: *(To STARBRIGHT.)* We best get going.

EFFIE: Hold up. How 'bout you stay, and we'll meet in the field out back in the morning and I'll work you a little.

JOYCE: I'll set you on the right course.

CASSIDY: I just— I don't have money for a coach. My Gran always coached me.

EFFIE: Won't cost ya.

CASSIDY: Um, really? Why not?

BB: …We don't need money.

CASSIDY: Why would you coach me, then?

EFFIE: 'Cause I know what it takes to win.

CASSIDY: But why me?

JOYCE and EFFIE look at each other.

EFFIE: 'Cause…

JOYCE: 'Cause…'cause… 'Cause you got loads of potential to be a star.

EFFIE: 'Cause once ya start getting off yer horse's head, you'll start moving up.

BB: Horse could use some coaching too. She's gotta come into the gate calm.

(To STARBRIGHT.) Swish swish.

STARBRIGHT: Swish swish.

JOYCE: I can work on your style.

EFFIE: *(To CASSIDY.)* Might wanna reconsider that particular offer…

BB:	Now Effie, play fair.
EFFIE:	No rules to this bet.
CASSIDY:	Bet?
JOYCE:	Um—
EFFIE:	Bet you can win. But you gotta have the desire ta win.
JOYCE:	Listen to me and you'll be a household name.
EFFIE:	Listen to me and I can help get you ta top of the list.
BB:	I'll help Starbright feel peaceful at the gate.
STARBRIGHT:	Peeeace.
CASSIDY:	I—uh—I don't—
JOYCE:	Wouldn't yer Gran want ya to shoot for yer dreams?
EFFIE:	See yer plans through?
CASSIDY:	I don't know.
EFFIE:	You gonna cowgirl up or get in the truck?
CASSIDY:	What do you think, Starry?
STARBRIGHT:	Uhhhhhhh huuuuh…
BB:	Swish swish.
STARBRIGHT:	Swish swish. Yeaaaah.
BB:	Yeaaah.
CASSIDY:	We're in, we're in.
EFFIE:	Atta girl. Now, get a good long sleep tonight.
JOYCE:	Gotta get yer beauty rest.

BB: We'll see you both in the morning. *(To STARBRIGHT.)* Swish swish.

STARBRIGHT: Swish swish.

EFFIE: Crack-a-dawn.

CASSIDY: We'll be ready.

They walk off.

CASSIDY: Crack-a-dawn. All them times Gran and I woke up early to train, do chores and open the barn. Stand there, feel the warmth of the sun coming up...Then run patterns in the pen.

STARBRIGHT: Awwwww.

CASSIDY: Gran useta say it don't matter what happens in the arena, long as we have each other, it's enough. Now she's gone and it's just us.

STARBRIGHT: Waaaaaaah.

CASSIDY: All the things I gotta do on my own. All the things I have to learn without her. Is this crazy?

STARBRIGHT: Huh huh.

CASSIDY: To think we might be able to get to the CRC?

STARBRIGHT: Yaaaaaa.

CASSIDY: Anything's gotta be better than going back to that empty house. Too lonely.

STARBRIGHT: Nuzzle nuzzle.

CASSIDY: Nuzzle nuzzle. Yer my blanket, Star, only family in the world.

CASSIDY hugs STARBRIGHT.

Scene 4

Morning. GODDESSES in the field.

JOYCE: Feels good to help out a young cowgirl. *(Beat.)* Good on ya, BB.

BB: Thank you, Joyce.

EFFIE: Yer not as dumb as ya look.

BB: Thank you, Effie.

EFFIE: Don't get too big on yerself. But the question is, will Joyce help or hinder our cowgirl?

JOYCE: BB will see this goddess make a superstar.

EFFIE: Oh, BB already knows I'm the sure winner.

BB: No decisions till the end, goddesses.

EFFIE: What a stickler.

CASSIDY and STARBRIGHT show up. STARBRIGHT whinnies.

JOYCE: Morning!

EFFIE: Good, yer on time.

CASSIDY: Morning.

EFFIE: Alright, let's get cracking. Starbright goes with BB.

BB: *(To STARBRIGHT.)* Swish swish.

STARBRIGHT: Swish swish.

EFFIE: Cassidy stays with me—

JOYCE: And me.

EFFIE: I s'pose.

CASSIDY: I thought we were going to train?

EFFIE: You bet we are.

JOYCE: Get ready, cowgirl.

BB: C'mon, Starbright. Swish swish.

STARBRIGHT: Swish swish.

EFFIE: *(To CASSIDY.)* To start, I want ya ta tell me what you were thinking yesterday as you were making that run.

CASSIDY: Uh...I dunno...I guess I was worrying if we were going too slow and seemed like we were making too wide a turn and—

EFFIE: Stop right there. When you compete you gotta quiet yer mind. Just be in the present moment.

BB face to face with STARBRIGHT.

BB: Flip flop, Starbright.

STARBRIGHT: Flip flop.

BB and STARBRIGHT train.

JOYCE: *(To EFFIE.)* My turn. *(To CASSIDY.)* Here's your first lesson to stardom—fake it till you make it.

CASSIDY: Fake it?

JOYCE: You know how all them seasoned barrel racers seem like they're so confident?

CASSIDY: Yeah, and I was a wreck.

JOYCE: Once you been here a few times, you get real used to it. I was a nervous Nelly first time I came too.

CASSIDY: You were?

JOYCE: So, you know what I did? Faked being the most confident barrel racer in the world. And you know what? It worked.

EFFIE: Did it now?

CASSIDY: Fake it till I make it.

JOYCE: That's my girl.

EFFIE: Okey-doke, now fer some actual training. You gotta visualize the whole race before you go on. Visualize all day, visualize while you do chores, visualize while eating, visualize while sittin' on the can.

CASSIDY: Visualize the race.

EFFIE: You bet.

JOYCE: Back to the golden path to fame…Always exit the arena with pride and a smile —no matter how you do. Paste on that smile. Smash with style.

EFFIE: Hey cowgirl, ready for the real coaching, tricks that'll stick?

CASSIDY: Yes, ma'am.

EFFIE: Before you go on, say this: S.F.T. See a perfect run. Feel the wind blowing my hair. Trust I've done all I can do.

CASSIDY: S.F.T.

EFFIE: Days I forgot to say that were days I didn't win.

JOYCE: I remember them days, I was the one winning

EFFIE: The only days—

JOYCE: Oh Effie, we all know that's not true

EFFIE: S.F.T. Now. Test. What's that stand for?

CASSIDY: S.F.T. See a perfect run. Feel the wind blowing my hair. Trust I've done all I can do.

BB: Now—horse tips for humans. You can't make a twelve-hundred-pound animal do something, you have to ask her.

EFFIE: Yer horse has no whoa—

JOYCE: She's all go, all the time.

BB: So, deep breaths.

STARBRIGHT: Breeeathe.

EFFIE: Horse has got it down. Now can the horse's cowgirl get it?

CASSIDY: Breeeathe.

BB: Good girl, Starry, here's a little sugar for you.

BB gives her some sugar.

CASSIDY: Oh…I don't give Star sugar.

BB: She deserves a little treat. We've been workin' hard.

STARBRIGHT: Suuuugar.

CASSIDY: Just this once. I don't want her getting used to it.

BB: There, you sweet thing. Now you gonna show off what you learned?

STARBRIGHT: Yeeeeah.

BB: Atta girl. Perseverance will serve you well.

JOYCE: So will a good mascara.

CASSIDY: My Gran used to say there's only one thing to do if you fall off your horse—get back on 'im.

EFFIE: That's the right attitude.

BB: Deep down we're what our grandmas created, same as almost every cowgirl I know.

JOYCE: My Grandma Hamilton was particular about how you make a bed.

EFFIE: If she's anything like you it's 'cause she twisted the sheets in the moonlight…

BB: Now, Effie…

EFFIE: Well, my Nan could swear a blue streak that could knock a buzzard off a shitwagon.

JOYCE: Well, that explains a lot.

BB: My Granny passed on her horse whispering to me.

CASSIDY: My Gran was my whole world, life without her is….

STARBRIGHT: Nuzzle nuzzle.

JOYCE: Oh hon, now you got us. You just need to step it up one more level.

JOYCE holds out a bright red lipstick

CASSIDY: ...I don't usually wear makeup.

JOYCE: *(Putting the lipstick on CASSIDY.)* Listen, cowgirl, the moment you ride into the arena, you want people to notice you, like a jolt, like a thunderbolt. You ready to be a star?

CASSIDY: Yeah. Not sure about the lipstick.

EFFIE: No kidding.

JOYCE: Winning look, ladies.

CASSIDY takes a big breath and smiles.

EFFIE: Alright, let's pack it in.

CASSIDY: Wait! We're not gonna run a pattern?

EFFIE: Nope. First lesson is all in your mind. Don't you worry, you'll have plenty of time in the arena goin' down the road to the CRC.

BB: Let's go. I'm starved.

JOYCE: Me too.

CASSIDY: Me too.

EFFIE: I could eat a horse.

STARBRIGHT whinnies.

EFFIE: Sorry.

Scene 5

ANNOUNCER: It is May, and the rodeo season has finally begun! Competitors are on what is known as "Goin' down the road"— doing the rodeo circuit in hopes of standing top 12 in Canada and qualifying for the Canadian Rodeo Championships.

Alright, Taber! I wanna hear ya! Let's get at 'er.

BB: Breathe.

JOYCE: Fake it till you make it.

EFFIE: S.F.T.

CASSIDY: And … go and go!

Two barrels get knocked down.

ANNOUNCER: Doggonit. Two barrels knocked down.

CASSIDY: Dammit.

STARBRIGHT: Flip flop.

EFFIE: Buck up, buttercup.

CASSIDY: Time 28.5 with penalty. Feel like everyone's laughing at me.

STARBRIGHT: Slush wush.

JOYCE: It's all part of the game.

ANNOUNCER: Alright, Kananaskis!

CASSIDY: And go!

ANNOUNCER: We are proud to host one of the earliest rodeos of the season.... This is your chance to see some of North America's greatest cowboys and cowgirls!

BB: But you gotta trust Starry is with you. *(To STARBRIGHT.)* Melt melt.

STARBRIGHT: Melt melt.

ANNOUNCER: C'mon, Cassidy.

Third barrel gets knocked down.

GODDESSES: OHHH.

CASSIDY: It's that third barrel. Locklear never knocks down her third barrel.

STARBRIGHT: Yuh yuh huh huh fa fa.

EFFIE: Stop comparing yerself.

STARBRIGHT: Yeeeaaaah.

ANNOUNCER: And it is June. Alright, Grand Prairie, kick up your boots at this community staple.

CASSIDY: What's the point? It's like we're on a losing streak.

STARBRIGHT: Huuuuuuuuuh.

JOYCE: Yer inching up. Folks are learning your name.

Third barrel is knocked down.

CASSIDY: I hate that third barrel!

STARBRIGHT: Wop yop wop yop.

EFFIE: Even when you lose, yer losing better.

ANNOUNCER: Alright, Sundrie. Rodeo in the beautiful West Country.

BB: You gotta trust.

JOYCE: You hafta lose to win.

ANNOUNCER: And it is July, otherwise known in the rodeo world as Cowboy Christmas!

Alright, Coronation!

CASSIDY: S.F.T. S.F.T. Fake it till you make it. Breathe.

STARBRIGHT: Breeeeathe.

CASSIDY: I did it! I beat that third barrel!

ANNOUNCER: Cassidy Clarkson is third in Strathmore!

STARBRIGHT: Whoa whoa!

BB: Go, Starbright!

EFFIE: Ya see? Ya got yer horse on the right lead.

JOYCE: Now yer starting to make money.

STARBRIGHT: Goooooooooo!

ANNOUNCER: And it's August. Alright, Pincher Creek!

CASSIDY: And go!

ANNOUNCER: We may take place in a small town, but we are a big pro rodeo. And Cassidy Clarkson places second!

JOYCE: We gotta real chance now.

ANNOUNCER: Cassidy Clarkson places first in Cochrane. This little lady is now ten places away from being the top 12 in Canada.

BB: Stomp Somp Romp, Starry!

STARBRIGHT: Stomp Somp Romp.

CASSIDY: I just can't... How many more rodeos do we have to do?

EFFIE: Till you make enough to qualify.

BB: You're both relaxed.

JOYCE: You are shining.

STARBRIGHT: Neeeeeiiiiigh.

EFFIE: So close I can taste it.

ANNOUNCER: Cassidy Clarkson is now just one place away from qualifying for the CRC in Red Deer.

EFFIE: Ah crap, forgot they moved the CRC to Red Deer.

ANNOUNCER: Will Cassidy Clarkson make the top 12 in Canada?

CASSIDY: I don't think we're going to make it.

STARBRIGHT: Fiiiiiiight.

BB: If you let Starbright lead.

JOYCE: If you can just remember to smile.

EFFIE: If you get yer hands figured out.

ANNOUNCER: And Cassidy Clarkson is standing twelve in Canada! She is going to the Canadian Rodeo Championships!

STARBRIGHT: Woooooooooot.

CASSIDY: I can't believe it, we did it!

STARBRIGHT: Swish swish!

EFFIE: I'm on fire again.

JOYCE: I'm shining again.

BB: Feels like old times.

CASSIDY: CRC, here we come!!

Scene 6

Canadian Rodeo Championships. CASSIDY and STARBRIGHT in the alley, waiting to go on.

CASSIDY: The Canadian Rodeo Championships. Oh Star, feel like I'm gonna barf. Did you see that girl that cut in front of us before we got here? Didn't even look at us. None of them looked at us. They've all been here before. They look so relaxed. They all got such big rigs too. Took me like fifteen minutes to even find the bathroom. Big crowd, biggest ever. Oh god. Oh Star. I can't barf, not here. Biggest day ever.

STARBRIGHT: Boooom. Baaaaam. No booom bam. Wham slam.

CASSIDY: Yeah, the music is too loud.

ANNOUNCER: Alright, Red Deer! Day one of the Canadian Rodeo Championships Ladies' Barrel Racing. The CRC brings together world-class athletes, both human and animal, in a weeklong celebration of rodeo and the rebellious freedom of the western lifestyle that lives strong in Alberta and beyond. Let's see how our twelve cowgirls do!

Amazing lineup of ladies at the back of the alley. Spurs clacking stirrups. Legs shaking. White knuckling. Butterflies in their bellies. So we need you to help them. Here's where we need ya ta make a lotta noise.

Audience cheers. The GODDESSES appear.

EFFIE: Holy moly. I'm blinded by yer shirt.

CASSIDY: Yeah, it's not really me, but —

JOYCE: She looks fantastic.

EFFIE: Shoulda known. Now yer all set. Go in there and just be, just do.

CASSIDY: Just be, just do.

BB: Keep yer ears open for me.

STARBRIGHT: Swish swish.

JOYCE: Smile and streak.

CASSIDY: Feel like I'm gonna barf…oh god, I'm gonna barf—

EFFIE: Hold yer breakfast, cowgirl.

CASSIDY: Oh god, I don't belong.

JOYCE: You do. Just imagine that one person in the stands, the only one who counts. Do it for them.

BB: Breathe.

CASS/STAR: Breeeeathe.

ANNOUNCER: And last up is Cassidy Clarkson on her horse Starbright to try to win that gold buckle. It's Cassidy Clarkson's first time at the CRC, so let's help her remember it!

CASSIDY: *(To STARBRIGHT.)* Let's do this for Gran.

STARBRIGHT: Graaaan.

ANNOUNCER: Alright, Cassidy, get it on, get it on. Everybody get loud. C'mon, sit down. Atta girl.

CASSIDY: And go and go.

STARBRIGHT: Raaaace raaaace.

BB: Here they come!

GODDESSES: Rate, rate, turn the perfect circle, first barrel…

ANNOUNCER: That is a beautiful number one barrel. That should dictate the success of the run.

EFFIE: She's riding well.

BB: She's letting Starry lead…

JOYCE: Turn the perfect circle. Turn the perfect circle.

GODDESSES: Second barrel…

EFFIE: See the pocket, the pocket!

JOYCE: She's shining.

ANNOUNCER: Number two just as good, now down to the third barrel.

BB: Leave it up, leave it up!

ANNOUNCER: C'mon, Canada. Cassidy is lookin' good.

GODDESSES: Third barrel…

BB: Star is flying. Flying—

JOYCE: Keep it up now. Keep it up.

EFFIE: Inside leg, inside leg.

Celebration.

ANNOUNCER: Thatta girl. See how fast, she's gonna get it done.

JOYCE: Love when the crowd roars.

EFFIE: Turning barrels Effie style.

BB: Starry can ride a hole in the wind.

ANNOUNCER: Look at that run home. Cassidy Clarkson must've had Lucky Charms for breakfast, on her first time at the Canadian Rodeo Championships. Let's see how she fared… And it's 14 point 627 for Cassidy Clarkson to go to the lead! You know the game, the louder you cheer, the quicker she can hear. Nicely done, Cassidy. Guess we'll see this new gal celebrating her win at the cab tonight.

GODDESSES celebrate.

BB: They won, they won!!

EFFIE: Pretty slick ride.

JOYCE: Weren't we stunning?

EFFIE: We got it done. Jesus Murphy, felt like my first time at the CRC.

BB: Today, we are true cowgirl goddesses.

JOYCE: I was shaking in my sequins.

BB: My heart was pounding so loud. They sure done us proud.

JOYCE: What a win.

EFFIE: Haven't felt a rush like this in years.

BB: Maybe this is a good time to tell her about the bet?

Beat.

JOYCE: Tell her about the bet?

EFFIE: Not on yer life.

JOYCE: We can't cloud her shining moment.

BB: Shouldn't she know?

EFFIE: She don't need ta know.

JOYCE: Will interrupt her flow, dull her glow.

EFFIE: Case closed.

CASSIDY comes up to them.

CASSIDY: Holy cow, holy moly—I just beat Lisa Locklear!

STARBRIGHT: Yaaaaaaa!

JOYCE: You were a dream to behold.

CASSIDY: I can't believe we won!

STARBRIGHT: Creeeeamed. Scheeeemed. Dreeeeaamed.

CASSIDY: We did, didn't we? We creamed it.

EFFIE: We gave 'em a show.

JOYCE: Did you hear all them people cheering?

BB: *(To STARBRIGHT.)* You brought it home for us, fly girl.

STARBRIGHT: Flyyyyyy.

BB nuzzles STARBRIGHT.

EFFIE: Hit the hay. We'll see you tomorrow morning.

CASSIDY: What?

EFFIE: Training at dawn.

CASSIDY: Wait. That's it? Don't I get to celebrate?

BB: Sure! You can celebrate with Starbright.

STARBRIGHT: Neiiigh yaaay.

CASSIDY: But look at all them cowgirls headed to the cab, they didn't even win.

EFFIE: We gotta keep our head in the game.

JOYCE: Job doesn't end in the arena. After a win, I always made sure my face was seen at the dance — just an hour, then got my beauty sleep.

CASSIDY: Sounds good to me.

STARBRIGHT: Neeigh neeigh, staay staay.

BB: Just cuddle with yer horse tonight. That's what I always did.

EFFIE: If we wanna win the week? We gotta just do our job, keep visualizing for tomorrow's race, and get a solid night's sleep.

JOYCE: Well…I won buckles and danced pretty at the cabs. I always liked to consort with my fans.

CASSIDY: You think I have fans?

JOYCE: Big win like this? I know it.

EFFIE: Fans can see us in the arena, where we earn our status.

CASSIDY: But it's like nothing special happened. You wanted me to win, and I won.

EFFIE: That's the work of an athlete. We don't coast on one win. Can't get all puffed up.

CASSIDY: So, back to my rig, alone, again.

EFFIE: You bet. Be a jockey, do yer work.

CASSIDY: I'm sick of being lonely.

JOYCE: Just one hour won't hurt her.

BB: Stay with Starbright, give her some sugar.

STARBRIGHT: Yaaaah, sugaaaar.

CASSIDY: I told you, I don't give Starbright sugar.

STARBRIGHT: Sweeeet.

CASSIDY: C'mon Star, I can go out for one hour. I don't feel like cooping up in the rig like we always do. I need a life outside of us.

STARBRIGHT: Sneeeeze, wheeeeeze, pleeeease.

EFFIE: Yer both athletes.

CASSIDY: It's not a big deal. I'm too excited to sleep. *(To STARBRIGHT.)* BB will get you to the rig.

She walks off. BB takes STARBRIGHT.

STARBRIGHT: Steeeeeeel meeeetal.

BB: Breeeathe, Starry, breathe.

Scene 7

At the bar. JED is sitting at the bar. CASSIDY bursts through the door, strides over to the bar, and sits next to JED. EFFIE is serving. JOYCE and BB sit nearby.

EFFIE: Whatcha want?

CASSIDY: How'd you get here?

EFFIE: You want a drink or not?

CASSIDY: Yer not my chaperone.

EFFIE: If you don't wanna drink, take the high road outta here.

CASSIDY: Jack Daniels, neat.

EFFIE: One fer the road.

JOYCE leans down the bar.

JOYCE: Pour her some water too. Hydrate!

CASSIDY: Jesus.

BB: Will keep you steady.

CASSIDY: Thought you were hosing Starbright.

BB: Already done, she's in the field.

JOYCE: One hour.

EFFIE: Tick tock, stay on the clock.

BB: Starry's waiting.

CASSIDY joins JED at his table.

CASSIDY: I'm sitting here, okay?

JED: Okay. That Jack Daniels?

CASSIDY: Yeah, so?

JED: Nice choice.

CASSIDY: Uh, thanks.

JED: Not many girls drink whisky water.

CASSIDY: It's what my Gran always drank.

JED: Yer a can chaser, right?

CASSIDY: Barrel racer. Top of the list today.

JED: Yeah? Me too. Sittin' first—still a lot of rodeo left though. Calves were pretty fresh tonight. I didn't have the best one—kicked some. Lotta fast times here, lotta guys tie 'em fast. Beat 'em tonight though. Goin ta Arizona soon.

CASSIDY: I'll buy you a cocktail to celebrate.

JED: What?

CASSIDY: Just kidding. Whatcha drinking, Bud?

CASSIDY pulls out a twenty bill, calls out to EFFIE.

CASSIDY: I'll take another. And get the cowboy here a Bud.

JED: I can buy my own drink.

CASSIDY: I just bought you one.

JED: Next round on me.

CASSIDY: I won big today. Beat Lisa Locklear.

JED: Who's that?

CASSIDY: You don't know Lisa Locklear?

JED: Don't follow can chasers.

CASSIDY: She's a three-time champion.

JED: I beat Tuf Cooper…one time.

CASSIDY: Who's that?

JED: You don't know Tuf Cooper?

CASSIDY: 'Course. Everyone knows Tuf Cooper. 'Cause he's a cowboy.

EFFIE: Bingo.

JOYCE: Oooh, she's being a spitfire…

BB: She's charged, alright.

EFFIE serves the drinks.

EFFIE: Don't expect ya to be chasing these ones down. Slow now.

JED: Yes, ma'am. *(To CASSIDY.)* Look, barrel racing was just made up by ladies so's you could get in the arena. Roping goes way back to the dark ages.

CASSIDY: Cowgirls go way back too.

JED: Not can chasing though.

CASSIDY: Last gymkhana, I roped and got a 9.2. That would place me with you.

JED: Must have had some wimpy calf. 120-pound girl can't compete with me.

CASSIDY: 150. Bet I can finish a Bud before you.

JED: Don't think so.

CASSIDY calls out to EFFIE.

CASSIDY: I'll take another Bud. *(To JED.)* Get ready.

JED: Oh, I'm ready.

CASSIDY: So you think.

JED: Good luck, cowgirl.

EFFIE brings her one, disapprovingly.

CASSIDY: Start a tab.

EFFIE: Can't do that.

CASSIDY: Uh, yeah, you can.

EFFIE: Closing up early tonight.

CASSIDY: Door said two am.

EFFIE: No self-respecting cowgirl stays out till two.

JOYCE: Home by nine, looking fine.

BB: Poor Starry…

JED pulls out a bill.

JED: Don't worry, I got this.

CASSIDY: How 'bout, you pay if you lose.

JED: Sweet deal for me. *(Sticks out his hand.)* Jed.

CASSIDY holds up her beer.

CASSIDY: Ready, Jed? One two three, drink.

CASSIDY and JED chug.

JOYCE: Chug chug chug! Keep your throat open!

BB: Joyce!

JOYCE: I used to chug with the best of 'em.

CASSIDY slams her empty beer can down first.

CASSIDY: How much did you say you weighed?

EFFIE takes his bill.

JED: Yer something, alright. How come I haven't seen you before?

CASSIDY: I don't usually come to the cabs.

JED: Why not? Can chasers are always in the corner cackling.

CASSIDY: Usually I just hang out with my horse, she's the best company.

JED: You can chasers baby yer horses.

CASSIDY: Made her myself.

JED: You don't say. *(To EFFIE.)* Two more.

EFFIE: Sold out.

EFFIE turns her back. JED takes a flask out of his jacket.

JED: Cheers.

JED takes a drink and then passes the flask to CASSIDY.

CASSIDY: Hurray, hurray!
First day of May.

Outdoor squealin'

Starts today.

Cheers.

CASSIDY drinks and hands back the flask.

JED: Ha ha! Where'd you learn that?

CASSIDY: My Gran.

JED: Yer Gran taught you that?

CASSIDY: She loved bein' facetious.

JED: What's that, that— facetious.

CASSIDY: Facetious?

JED: Why're you talkin' like that?

CASSIE: Sayin' facetious?

JED: What's it mean then?

CASSIDY: Can chasers get their high school diplomas.

JED: What, you think I'm stupid?

CASSIDY: Look it up.

JED: C'mon.

CASSIDY: Sarcastic.

JED: Well, why didn't you just say sarcastic?

CASSIDY: 'Cause it don't have the same meaning.

JED: Then why'd you say it did?

CASSIDY: And yer not even a bulldogger. Least they got knocked head as an excuse.

JOYCE: Haha, take him down a size!

BB: She can sure dish out.

EFFIE: He's trippin' on his lip.

CASSIDY: *(To GODDESSES.)* A little room here, ladies?

JED: *(To CASSIDY.)* Yeah, you won at all them estrogen fests this year, made some money and now you think yer something.

CASSIDY: And what if I am something? You ever barrel race?

JED: Only if I'm wearin' a hot pink bikini.

CASSIDY: Screw you.

JED: All you barrel racers are crazy. And yer horses are crazy. All jumped up, keyed up. Yer all crazy.

CASSIDY: I got more skill, more precision and killer instincts. That's why I'm here.

JED: Candy in a can chaser.

CASSIDY: Like to see you try running the barrels.

JED: Sure, I'll ride like you, monkey humpin' a football.

CASSIDY: Hey! Cowgirls work harder than anyone, but especially cowboys. You just wanna get down the road, nothing else matters but the next rodeo. But yer broke, 'cause you spent all yer money, and you don't have any other aspirations at all, other than being a cowboy. And you wake up each morning, greasy, smelly and hung over the back of yer truck.

EFFIE: Goshdarn right.

JED: You girls can't back a truck and trailer to save yer life. You give attitude about ground conditions, and go through farriers like underwear.

CASSIDY: I'll be heading to Calgary come July.

JED: I been to Calgary six times.

CASSIDY: Sad rodeo clown.

JED: Pumped-up prima donna. Let's see how you do come tomorrow.

CASSIDY: Let's see how you do.

JED: You'll be tuck-tailin' it home.

EFFIE: She should tuck-tail it to her rig.

CASSIDY: You'll be the sore loser again.

JED: Hope you have a good life.

CASSIDY: You bet I will.

JED: 'Kay then.

CASSIDY: 'Kay.

CASSIDY storms to the door. JOYCE AND BB follow her.

JOYCE: Perfect note to leave on.

BB: Starbright's lonely…

EFFIE: Get get get!

Two-step begins.

CASSIDY looks at the GODDESSES. She walks back to the bar.

BB: Uh oh!

JOYCE: Can we rope her back?

CASSIDY: *(Starts to dance.)* Turn it up! *(To JED.)* Bet you can't two-step worth nothin'.

EFFIE: Jesus Murphy.

JED: Guess what, I can too.

CASSIDY: Like, a proper two-step?

JED: Yeah. Mom taught us.

CASSIDY: Let's see then.

They dance. JED can do a proper two-step. CASSIDY is impressed but tries not to show it.

CASSIDY: Hoping to do some trailer-hoppin' tonight?

JED: Nah. *(Beat.)* You?

CASSIDY: Depends. Looking for the right cowboy. *(Beat.)* Them bulldoggers are real men. You timies are boys.

JED: We're not boys.

CASSIDY: Total mama's boys.

JED: You don't strike me as the type to trailer-hop anyway.

CASSIDY: How's it work? With them buckle bunnies.

JED: Whatcha mean?

CASSIDY: How do you tell 'em apart? How do you choose?

JED: I dunno…the one with a twinkle in her eye.

CASSIDY: She ask about the name of yer horse?

JED: Nope. Never.

CASSIDY: What's yer horse's name?

JED: Tweeter.

CASSIDY: What kinda stupid name is that? Tweeter.

JED: What's yers?

CASSIDY: Starbright.

JED: Ha. You must have been some frilly girl to name her that.

CASSIDY: Bet you wouldn't know what to do if you got on her to make a run.

JED: Bet I could do it with my eyes closed and hands behind my back.

CASSIDY: That so. *(Beat.)* So then what?

JED: Whatcha talking about?

CASSIDY: After the twinkle.

JED: Well, usually we inch toward each other.

CASSIDY: She get ya to sit on her lap like this?

She pulls him over to sit on her lap.

EFFIE: Son of a biscuit.

BB: She's racing, reelin'.

JOYCE: Love me a cowgirl who takes charge.

JED: Uh, no. Usually the other way around.

He tries to get off, but she keeps him there. CASSIDY turns him around and kisses him.

JED: Nicely done….

JED moves in closer.

EFFIE: Okay now, time to hit the hay….

BB: Star's waitin ta turn in.

JOYCE: Beauty sleep…

CASSIDY: I'm heading back to my rig now, okay?

EFFIE: See ya crack-a-dawn tomorrow.

CASSIDY: Night, night, ladies.

CASSIDY goes to leave, checks to see that the GODDESSES aren't listening and turns to JED.

CASSIDY: Meet me at the warm-up pen in ten.

Scene 8

The warm-up pen. CASSIDY is waiting with STARBRIGHT.

STARBRIGHT: Huff huff wanna rig.

CASSIDY: Yeah, soon, Starry.

STARBRIGHT: Huh huh nuh nuh. Sweet sweet.

CASSIDY: C'mon, you can have some sweet sweet when we get back, okay?

STARBRIGHT: Suuuuugar.

CASSIDY: No sugar.

STARBRIGHT: Huh huh.

JED shows up.

JED: Hey, spitfire. *(Looks at STARBRIGHT.)* You brought yer horse?

STARBRIGHT: Nuh uh nuh uh.

CASSIDY: This is Starbright.

STARBRIGHT: Whiiiiiine wanna turrrrn ouuuuut.

CASSIDY: C'mon, Star. Hold up for a bit.

JED: Hey, girl.

STARBRIGHT: Sluff sluff gruff gruff guff guff.

CASSIDY: Get on her, cowboy.

STARBRIGHT: Whhhhhhaaaa?

JED: Uh—Thought we were gonna have some fun.

CASSIDY: This is fun. Yer turn to make a run. I'm not even gonna make you close your eyes or tie your hands behind your back.

JED: What?

CASSIDY: Let's see how you chase cans. If you think it's so easy.

JED: Right now? That's why you wanted to meet me here?

CASSIDY: Chicken?

JED: No.

He looks at STARBRIGHT.

STARBRIGHT: Huh huh.

CASSIDY: Call yer bluff?

JED: I'll do some can chasing.

JED starts to get on STARBRIGHT, but she backs up.

STARBRIGHT: Nuh uh nuh uh.

JED: I don't think yer horse likes me.

CASSIDY: Quit yer stalling and get on her.

JED gets on.

STARBRIGHT: Huh huh huh huh.

JED: Alright, let's go, girl.

STARBRIGHT balks.

JED: C'mon now. *(To CASSIDY.)* She's not letting me go.

STARBRIGHT: Huh huh.

CASSIDY: Hey hey! Starry.

STARBRIGHT: Awwwwww. Shucks shucks.

STARBRIGHT runs out of the alley.

CASSIDY: And go and go. And he's off. Comin in down the alley. Let's get going there, cowboy, fast now. Oh, that's a sloppy turn. And the first barrel is down. Five-second penalty, cowboy.

STARBRIGHT: Huff puff rough rough.

CASSIDY: And he's coming to the second barrel.

JED: C'mon now, turn nice and smooth for me.

STARBRIGHT: Nuff nuff rough stuff.

CASSIDY: Dogonnit! Second barrel's down! And coming down the third barrel now. Keep yer pink bikini on, cowboy!

STARBRIGHT: Slick sick saddle trick.

STARBRIGHT makes JED's leg hit the third barrel.

JED: Owww!

CASSIDY: Third barrel's still standing! Now, run 'er to home! Look at him starfish! And time is 18.5 but with the ten-second penalty that comes in at 28.5 for our cowboy. You can see why the ladies don't let the gents run their horses too often.

STARBRIGHT: Sneeze wheeze please.

CASSIDY: Well, least you left one up.

JED: Ah, c'mon.

CASSIDY walks up to JED.

CASSIDY: So.

JED: Yeah.

CASSIDY: Good thing you had Starbright under you. Not Tweeter.

JED: Hey now.

CASSIDY: Who knows what kind of a wreck you two woulda made.

STARBRIGHT: Steeep steeep wreeeck.

JED: Yeah yeah, go on, make fun of me, I know yer dying to.

CASSIDY: Well, what can I say...you looked like a monkey humping a football.

JED: Guess I deserve that.

CASSIDY: Guess you do.

JED: Y'all make it look easy.

CASSIDY: So he admits it.

JED: Yes, ma'am.

STARBRIGHT: Nuff nuff stuff huff.

CASSIDY: Okay, Starry. Let's go tuck in.

She turns to go.

JED: Yer leaving?

CASSIDY: I gotta put Starry to bed.

JED: But we gotta celebrate. I left one barrel up.

CASSIDY: Starry gets upset—

JED: What'd I say about babying yer horse? She'll be fine. One more drink for the rodeo star.

STARBRIGHT: Whhhha?? Tuuuuuck in.

JED: Didn't you say you were top of the heap today?

STARBRIGHT: Nooooo. Riiiig. Nooow.

JED: You beat Lisa Locklear.

STARBRIGHT: Huh nuh uh nuh uh.

JED: Yer a champion.

STARBRIGHT: RIIIG. NOW.

JED: No more babying, cowgirl. Are you a champion or not?

CASSIDY: I am a champion. *(To STARBRIGHT.)* Just this one time. I'll be back before you know it. You stay here, okay?

STARBRIGHT: Gruuuuuntle gruuuunt. Huh huh.

CASSIDY and JED leave.

STARBRIGHT: Snuuuufle gruuuumble. Huh huh. Ruuuumble raaa-ttle…

On her own, STARBRIGHT sulks. Gets herself in a fury and injures herself. She whimpers and sulks.

End of Act I.

ACT TWO

Scene 1

Morning. STARBRIGHT in the warm-up pen, with a hung head.

CASSIDY: *(Offstage.)* STARRY!

CASSIDY bursts into the arena. She rushes up to STARBRIGHT.

CASSIDY: Star, I'm so sorry.

STARBRIGHT: Huff huff snuff snuff.

CASSIDY: I fell asleep. I'm sorry, okay? Yer okay.

STARBRIGHT: Rough rough.

CASSIDY: C'mon, be easy on me, I got a splitting headache.

STARBRIGHT: Sluff sluff gruff gruff guff guff. Huh huh.

JED comes in holding CASSIDY's coat.

CASSIDY: C'mon, girl.

JED: Hey, Starbright.

STARBRIGHT: Huh huh huh.

JED: Still doesn't like me.

STARBRIGHT: Nuh uh.

CASSIDY: She's just mad at me.

JED: Horses are resilient. It's one night. She's fine.

CASSIDY: Gonna be a rough day.

JED: *(Hands over her coat.)* You forgot this. Wasn't sure I'd see you again. But maybe I could. Sometime. Uh, you free? Tonight?

CASSIDY: Uh—

JED: *(Beat.)* I'd really like to give 'er a try.

STARBRIGHT: Reeeek.

CASSIDY: Uh, I gotta deal with Starbright. C'mon, Starry, time to train.

STARBRIGHT: Nuh uh.

CASSIDY: Don't pull that. Nuzzle nuzzle.

STARBRIGHT: Neiggggh Noooo.

CASSIDY: Pout all you want then.

JED: *(Looking at STARBRIGHT.)* Is she walking funny?

CASSIDY: What? No. Look, we gotta get ready. Hope this doesn't throw her off. Come on, girl.

JED: Wait a sec. I got something that'll help.

JED takes a vial out of his coat and hands it to her.

JED: Frog juice. Give it to her before the race, she'll be raring to go.

CASSIDY: Dermorphin?

JED: This'll give her a great edge.

CASSIDY: Isn't it cheating?

JED: Nah, we all use it. Every cowboy's got some in his rig.

CASSIDY: Is it safe?

JED: One run on that won't hurt her. Twenty seconds all told.

Beat.

You gotta do what you gotta do to help yer horse get a leg up.

CASSIDY: On the farm, my Gran never gave anything to her horses 'cept bute.

JED: Are you some old lady back on the farm? No, Yer at the CRC, cowgirl, this is the real deal. This is what winners do.

CASSIDY: I don't know.

JED: You wanna win, doncha?

The GODDESSES enter. CASSIDY pockets the vial.

EFFIE: So here you are.

CASSIDY: Uh, I was practising here for a change.

BB: We got worried.

JOYCE: We've been looking all over for you.

CASSIDY: Sorry.

EFFIE spots JED.

EFFIE: You again.

JED: *(Tips his hat.)* Ladies.

EFFIE: Hit the road, Jack.

JED: Yes, ma'am.

JED slinks out.

JOYCE: *(To CASSIDY.)* Yer a mess.

CASSIDY: But I'm in my sequins, right?

JOYCE: You should always be prepared, have yer game face on.

EFFIE: You always gotta have yer A-game.

CASSIDY: I do have my A-game.

EFFIE: Alright, let's go. We're gonna run a pattern.

BB walks over to the knocked-over barrel. It is dented.

BB: Barrel's bashed up. Starry? *(Looks at STARBRIGHT.)* What's up with Starbright?

CASSIDY: She's fine. I'm fine. Everybody's fine, right?

BB: *(To STARBRIGHT.)* Starry?

STARBRIGHT: Huh huh.

CASSIDY: She's still holding a grudge from me going out.

BB: No, she's packing a leg, look.

CASSIDY: She's just trying to get sympathy. She knows if she does that, she looks more hard done by. Not the first time she's pulled this.

BB: You groom her?

CASSIDY: 'Course.

EFFIE: Alright. Up you get. Today we're gonna focus on the pocket.

BB: Trot her round the barrel first, to get her mood back on track.

CASSIDY and STARBRIGHT trot around the barrel.

EFFIE: Tight now. Yer being sloppy.

CASSIDY: We just started.

EFFIE: Gonna use that as an excuse?

BB: Starry? You okay?

STARBRIGHT: Huh nuh huh.

BB: Is Starbright moving different?

CASSIDY: Like I said—

BB: Maybe I should look at her hooves.

CASSIDY: Let us get warmed up.

BB: But she seems—

EFFIE: Now gimme a giant circle. Uh huh uh huh— Tighten 'er, ya got me?

CASSIDY and STARBRIGHT start to circle.

BB: Don't rush, don't get Starry too hot.

JOYCE: Look at the top of the barrel.

EFFIE: Lower yer hands.

BB: Slow down.

JOYCE: Softer.

EFFIE: Too sharp. Yer still in a fog. Both of ya.

CASSIDY: We're trying.

EFFIE: We're just doin exercises, same as always.

BB: Breathe, Starbright. Breathe.

JOYCE: Yer both low energy.

CASSIDY: I just need a minute.

CASSIDY jumps down and walks STARBRIGHT off to the side, bends over trying not to throw up. They watch her.

EFFIE: Okey-doke. Last night you rode your adrenaline rush high as ya could. But in the middle of the CRC, ya can't get too high or too low.

JOYCE: You gotta learn to take your wins as well as your losses.

BB: Ride the middle ground.

EFFIE: So keep yer eye on the end game. Yer a rookie, and ya got a steep learning curve ahead of ya. I know what it's like in the middle of the week here, ya can't rest on yer laurels. Ya gotta stay on task, play the long game. My first time here, I did nothing but ride, eat and sleep.

BB: I always treated me and my horse the same. Took care of us both.

JOYCE: I sparkled in the spotlight but made sure I got my eight hours with my sleep mask.

CASSIDY: I will from now on, promise

EFFIE: 'Kay then. Get some water and we'll start this morning over proper in five minutes.

JOYCE: And brush that hair smooth.

BB: Wait—what's wrong with Starbright? Look at her.

STARBRIGHT is bobbing her head vigorously.

STARBRIGHT: Huh nuh huh nuh.

CASSIDY: What? C'mon, Starry.

STARBRIGHT: Not not. Rot rot rot.

BB: Oh my goddess. Thought she seemed off, compensating with her other leg.

STARBRIGHT: Huh nuh noooo rooooock shoooooock croooock.

STARBRIGHT starts to kneel down.

CASSIDY: Oh my god. Starry?

BB checks STARBRIGHT. Touches her leg. STARBRIGHT whimpers.

BB: Her leg is swollen.

CASSIDY: Oh, Star. We'll go cold hose, and wrap. C'mon, you'll feel so much better after the hose, wrapping will feel nice, okay? So nice and cool….

STARBRIGHT: Huh huh huh. Nooo niiiiight niiiiight.

BB: Think it's a tendon filling.

EFFIE: Dang-it.

JOYCE: She was fine yesterday. How could this happen?

Long beat.

CASSIDY: She spent the night outside.

BB: You left her out?

CASSIDY: I fell asleep.

BB: That's...that's...Oh, Starry.

Pause.

JOYCE: What a mess.

EFFIE: Well, that just tans my hide. Rule number one, ya don't leave yer horse out for the night.

JOYCE: What were you thinking?

BB: What happened, Starry?

CASSIDY: She was fine when I left her. *(To STARBRIGHT.)* Here's a treat, c'mon.

STARBRIGHT doesn't eat the treat.

How 'bout some sugar?

STARBRIGHT: Neighnooooo. Hoooooome.

BB: Poor thing.

STARBRIGHT: Quaaaaaake, aaaaaaache, shaaaaake.

CASSIDY: Star, Starry, it's okay, it's okay...

BB: Can't run Starry if she's sore.

EFFIE: Yer gonna need a new horse for tomorrow's run.

CASSIDY: What? No. Starry—Star, come on, buck up, buck up.

STARBRIGHT: Suuuuuck buuuuuuuuck huuuuuuck. Hoooooome.

CASSIDY: We can't go home now, Star.

BB: You hurt yer horse. She hasta rest. I'm taking her back to the rig.

BB and STARBRIGHT leave.

JOYCE: We'll find you a winner mount for tomorrow.

CASSIDY: She'll be better tomorrow.

EFFIE: But what if she's not?

CASSIDY: She has to be.

EFFIE: We'll get you the best. Just do a few practice rounds with the new horse, and then just hold on and ride.

CASSIDY: I can't do the final run without Starbright.

EFFIE: You liked winning yesterday?

CASSIDY: Yes.

EFFIE: Then listen. We helped ya beat Lisa Locklear, Nancy Sawyer, and all the rest of 'em. So what are ya willing to do to get that title? You think Starbright wants you sitting around all miserable? She wants ya to win. Ya gonna be some weepy, girlie sap because ya can't have things the way ya thought you would? Life don't work that way.

JOYCE: Slap on your face, paste on a smile, focus on the win.

EFFIE: You gonna stop now?

CASSIDY: No.

EFFIE: You wanna win this?

CASSIDY: Yes.

EFFIE: Good.

CASSIDY: I'm going to win.

JOYCE: That's the right attitude.

EFFIE: We'll get ya a new horse for tomorrow.

Scene 2

Morning. Training pen.

EFFIE: Alright. We got three of the best mounts around for you to try. First up we got Rebel.

REBEL enters.

Truly one of a kind. Rebel is a straighter-type horse. Runs hard, rates hard. He isn't a flashy horse, but he makes up his time with super-straight lines, and no wasted steps. He's all about getting the job done and done better than the rest. Get acquainted.

CASSIDY looks at REBEL.

REBEL: Wanna go. Wanna go.

CASSIDY: He's too hot.

EFFIE: You haven't even ridden him yet. Get on.

REBEL: Wanna go.

CASSIDY: See?

REBEL: Wanna go! Wanna run.

CASSIDY: He's too impatient.

REBEL: Wanna run!

CASSIDY: *(To REBEL.)* You gotta calm first. We're not gonna run yet.

REBEL: Need to run!

CASSIDY: Running comes later.

EFFIE: Trot him round a buncha times, that'll settle him.

REBEL: No. Wanna go.

CASSIDY: That means I'll have to do that before the race. And who knows how long it'll take him.

REBEL: Go fast.

EFFIE: Get on him and see. He's a dolt, but he runs so darn fast you'll be happy you made it without falling off.

REBEL: Not a dolt. Just fast.

EFFIE: Just give him a go.

REBEL: Wanna go breeze now.

CASSIDY: We won't work together.

EFFIE: Jesus Murphy. You haven't even tried him.

CASSIDY: I don't have time for a horse who tells me what to do.

REBEL: Just wanna eat grass.

Beat.

EFFIE: Fine. We'll try the next one. *(Calls out.)* Joyce. Yer up.

JOYCE comes in with MUFFIN.

JOYCE: This is Muffin. She is light in the mouth and loves to fly to the first barrel. As you can see, very appealing to the eye.

MUFFIN: Preeeeeeetty.

JOYCE: The bloodline Frenchman's Guy on her top side gives her rate and turn while the bloodline Truckle Feature Bunny Bid on the bottom side gives her the run. She's very turny and stays more flat with a rollback style. She's primed and ready to run.

CASSIDY: She's too heavy in the front end.

MUFFIN: Nooooo. Preeeeetty.

JOYCE: She's got a good shoulder. She's got a good hind end. Back legs. Good muscle.

MUFFIN: Yeeeeeah. Goooood.

CASSIDY: Too long gaskin muscle. Too big a dip in her back.

MUFFIN: Noooooo. Preeeeetty. Puuuuuuurfect.

JOYCE: Just get on her, and give her a run, lope a pattern. She knows what she's doing, won the CRC few years back. Just point and ride.

MUFFIN: Wiiiiiinner.

CASSIDY: I don't want anyone's sloppy seconds.

MUFFIN: Noooooooooot.

JOYCE: You don't have to keep her forever, just for tonight. Get up on her.

CASSIDY: She's not even looking at me.

MUFFIN: Dooooon't like.

JOYCE: Just hang on and ride her. She'll do the work for you, you'll both look mighty fine together.

CASSIDY: I can't. I can't ride her. I can't.

MUFFIN: Doooooon't liiike.

JOYCE: You don't even know her yet.

CASSIDY: She just feels wrong.

Beat.

BB: Okay, then. We got a last one for ya, real special, touched by the heavens, ya might say.

BB rides up on LOU.

BB: This is Lou.

LOU: Howdy.

BB: Lou is a four-wheel drive, easy, simple, let him do his job, and stay out of the way.

EFFIE: You hear that now?

CASSIDY: He's missing his left eye.

BB: He was born that way. Missing eye don't bother him at all. It's his secret ally. His one eye makes others pass him up, but he's fierce, won Calgary three times. Everything else is great, conformationally.

CASSIDY: No. I always ride a beautiful horse.

BB: But this is a blessed horse.

CASSIDY: I don't see it.

BB: You can sacrifice looks for an exceptional ride.

CASSIDY: No. I can't.

BB: This guy has a winning history. Trust that this horse can do. Look at his strong back. Low tail set. Built so he can get down on the ground for his turns. He'll do the job for you. Just hang on, stay out of the horse's way. Let him prove himself.

JOYCE: We're running out of time.

CASSIDY: I want the best.

BB: Lou is the best. And all ya done is look at him. Can't say no till you give him a try.

EFFIE: Choose Rebel, he's the fastest here.

CASSIDY: I need a beauty under me.

JOYCE: Then go with Muffin! Pretty as all heck in a wind picture.

CASSIDY: None of 'em are gonna work.

LOU: Okay.

LOU mopes away.

JOYCE: Cool your temper, cowgirl.

BB: This is no way for a champion to behave.

JOYCE: 'Specially a cowgirl, you gotta watch yerself here.

EFFIE: So pick one, get off yer high horse and on to one of them mounts.

CASSIDY: Stop pushing me. You three are on my back. Whining in my ear. Three mosquitos, buzzing. Buzz buzz, every day. I'm telling you they're not gonna work, so they're not gonna work.

JOYCE: We searched high and low for these horses.

BB: And you're not letting them horses show what they can do.

EFFIE: And yer being a snot. I thought you said you wanted to win, but yer not acting like a winner, a winner does whatever it takes ta win, it don't matter what.

CASSIDY: None of them suit me. They don't care about me. Without Starbright, I won't win.

BB: You can't ride a hurt horse.

EFFIE: Get that in yer friggin' noodle.

JOYCE: Fix that attitude, cowgirl.

BB: Starry has her own path to follow now. And it's not in the arena.

CASSIDY: It's Starbright or nothing.

EFFIE: *(To JOYCE.)* Guess the bet's off.

JOYCE: Guess so.

CASSIDY: What are you talking about?

EFFIE: Nothin'.

CASSIDY: No wait—what? What bet?

BB: We…

JOYCE: Made a bet.

CASSIDY: On what.

EFFIE: On you.

CASSIDY: Me?

JOYCE: You.

CASSIDY: What kind of bet?

EFFIE: To see if we could make a winner. We picked the worst of the worst—

JOYCE: Best of the worst—

BB: Cowgirl with the most potential.

EFFIE: Joke's on us.

CASSIDY: This was all a bet? I was the worst?

JOYCE: Best of the worst…We knew we could help you earn the title.

EFFIE: Just a question of who could get you there. Turns out, no one can.

CASSIDY: So, you were just playing with me. This whole time.

BB: No, we believed in you and Starry.

CASSIDY: I'm the only one who calls her Starry. *(To EFFIE.)* I won them races, not you, you keep trying to take all the credit, but it was me out there. *(To BB.)* Starbright is my horse, not yours. *(To JOYCE.)* I don't like being flashy and loud like you. *(To ALL.)* I'm not playing your ego game. You're nothing but a pack of liars. Star and I were fine before you came along with your stupid bet. Leave us alone.

CASSIDY runs off.

EFFIE: *(To JOYCE.)* Ya made her a diva just like you.

JOYCE: Oh, so yer the perfect role model? Yer a crusty cowgirl and she's learned yer crusty ways. Apple don't fall far from the tree.

EFFIE: You always were a bad sport.

JOYCE: Oh hooey, you been acting like this win was all yours.

EFFIE: I don't wanna help a diva.

BB: Way she treated them beautiful horses hurt my heart.

JOYCE: *(To EFFIE.)* Yer a bully and ya bullied her and that's why she snapped.

EFFIE: No, ma'am. This is on you, Joyce. If ya hadn't sent her sailing off to the cab to lose her head with that cowboy, none of this would have happened.

JOYCE: Don't you start on that. A cowgirl needs more than herself.

EFFIE: I never found anyone I liked more than me, and I did just fine.

JOYCE: She's not you, Effie.

EFFIE: She's not you either, Joyce. Dagnabbit. I really thought we had a chance.

JOYCE: So it's all over? Our lineage stops here?

EFFIE: Don't know, don't care.

BB: We shouldn't have made it a bet.

EFFIE: We shouldn't have come down here in the first place. Didja even think about the repercussions of goddesses meddling with humans?

BB: You're blaming me now?

EFFIE: Far as I see it, this whole plan is a load of horse crap.

BB: I don't regret meeting Starry.

EFFIE: Guess what? Starry would be fit as a fiddle right now, if ya hadn't interfered. You can blame yerself for that one.

BB: Yer a mean old bull, Effie.

BB runs off.

JOYCE: Never should have left the skybox.

EFFIE and JOYCE stomp off in different directions.

Scene 3

CASSIDY in the rig with STARBRIGHT.

CASSIDY: Oh Starry, them coaches got me the most stubborn horses. Didn't get me at all. I can't ride any of them—

STARBRIGHT: Huuuuh nuuuuuh.

CASSIDY: I can't trust them. One had a temper, another one barely looked at me.

STARBRIGHT: Whhhhaa? Huh huh nuh uh.

CASSIDY: I know. Can't trust anyone but you and Gran.

STARBRIGHT: Mush gush mush gush.

CASSIDY leans her head on STARBRIGHT's. Gives her a treat.

CASSIDY: If only Gran were here. She'd know what to do. She'd sit on that wooden milk stool and she'd set me on the ledge of the tack room, and we'd figure out what to do next.

STARBRIGHT: Huh huh huh huh.

CASSIDY: Gran wouldn't want us to give up now.

STARBRIGHT: Yaaaah. Huuuuh. Ride, slaaam dunk, yahhhh.

CASSIDY: Wait—

Rummages in her coat pocket and takes out the vial of Dermorphin.

CASSIDY: Jed said this Dermorphin could take care of your pain. Could you do one quick ride tonight?

STARBRIGHT: Yeaaaah.

CASSIDY: If this is what winners do…we should do it, right?

STARBRIGHT: Huh huh.

CASSIDY: Star and Cassidy, can't have one without the other. Just a little pinch.

CASSIDY injects the Dermorphin into Starbright. CASSIDY kisses STARBRIGHT.

CASSIDY: You alright?

STARBRIGHT: Huh huh yuh yuh.

CASSIDY: We win this, then everything was worth it. We belong together.

Scene 4

In the arena. Hard rocking music. Blasts of fire. CASSIDY on STARBRIGHT in the alley.

ANNOUNCER Ladies and gentlemen, nearly fifty thousand tickets have been sold this week. And close to 1.4 million dollars will be paid out overall. I want to take a moment for all of you to think about the significance of this day. Take a moment and have the freedom to dream. What would it be like? It all comes down to one final performance. A lifetime of dreaming will turn into a reality as our champions are crowned. So friends, do me a favour, will ya, let's get loud, and wish every contestant today the best of luck in the final round, at the CRC.

JOYCE and EFFIE arrive in the stands, BB is already there.

EFFIE: *(To JOYCE.)* Decided to come, didja?

JOYCE: Wasn't gonna miss it.

EFFIE: You seen Cassidy?

JOYCE: No. Did you?

EFFIE: No.

EFFIE/JOYCE: *(To BB.)* Did you?

BB; No. But I'm sure she came to her senses about Lou. That blessed horse can do.

EFFIE: Bet she figured Rebel was the best choice. Straight shooter horse, straight shooter win.

JOYCE: Oh no, she knows a pretty horse like Muffin will show her off the best and win her the CRC.

ANNOUNCER: Courage. Strength and determination. Today's the day to crown our Canadian champions. Today's the day that dreams will be realized. Championship Sunday.

This little lady has run away with the title, she's the leading money winner this week, and winning the average as well. Welcome to the one and only, Canadian Cassidy Clarkson.

CASSIDY runs out to the arena and tips her hat.

ANNOUNCER: She is so close, so very close. Alright, get back on yer horse, little lady. Ladies and gentlemen, we've come to love the horse Cassidy has brought to town, this buckskin with the fitting name of Starbright.

JOYCE: She didn't…

BB: She can't!

EFFIE: Son of a biscuit.

JOYCE: Maybe Starbright woke up better.

BB: Maybe she didn't, but she's running her anyway.

ANNOUNCER: I wantcha to help them!

Doors fly open.

STARBRIGHT: YAAAAAAA!

CASSIDY: Alright. Alright. This is it, this is really it. Can't wait to get out there. Feeling good now, right?

STARBRIGHT: Yaaaah wooo hooo ha!

CASSIDY: Haha! I knew you were good. Feeling strong?

STARBRIGHT: Stroooong!

CASSIDY: That's my girl.

ANNOUNCER: Alright. C'mon, Cassidy.

CASSIDY: And go!

CASSIDY and STARBRIGHT run in.

ANNOUNCER: And here they are, on the top of the ground. Okay, they're in.

C'mon, Cassidy, ride her like the wind. Yup, there it is, get around that first barrel tight and right. Nicely done. Now huurrry onto that second barrel. That is really the perfect turn…Now she's onto the third. That's right, good style. No knock down. Now throw the reins at her, Cassidy, let's go, little lady. She has been solid as a rock all week long. Help her home.

GODDESSES: Hustle!

STARBRIGHT streaks for home.

ANNOUNCER: The only thing I know for sure is who the fastest run of the round is, that's gonna be Cassidy Clarkson at 14. 603. She has won the Canadian title.

GODDESSES: Yee-haw!!!

ANNOUNCER: We'll see you at the—

STARBRIGHT falls and rolls over on her back, CASSIDY falls off. GODDESSES stand up.

STARBRIGHT: Whaaaaaaaa Haaaaaa Ahhhhhh.

ANNOUNCER: Wait, wait a moment, Starbright has fallen, bringing Cassidy down with her. They've won the Canadian title, but she's flipped on her back.

BB: No! No no no, Starry.

EFFIE: Hold up, she's hurt but she's not— I don't think she's—

JOYCE: What's happening? What's happening?

EFFIE: Can't tell.

BB: *(Covering her eyes.)* I can't look.

CASSIDY: Ohnononono. Starbright. You okay? Yer okay….

ANNOUNCER: C'mon …

STARBRIGHT: Roooooooarrrrr.

CASSIDY: Starbright, can you get up? What is it?

STARBRIGHT: Nooooo. Waaayyyy. Ouuutta here. Ya ya ya. Booones ache, shaaaake. Weeary wear, scare, paaain whip whap pit-ter pat-ter heeeave up heave peeve leave, ya yah uh huh uh huh uh huh.

CASSIDY: Starbright! Starbright…

STARBRIGHT: Groan moan, moon, snip snap barn hay dawn day, nooo saaay….

CASSIDY looks at STARBRIGHT. STARBRIGHT's leg is twisted.

ANNOUNCER: And she is down. Oh no. That horse is... That was a nasty fall for Cassidy Clarkson of Claresholm and her horse, Starbright. Ladies and gentlemen, this would be a very good time to take the kids out of the arena and get them some cotton candy. That's right. We got pink, we got blue. Run and get it, kids. We'll just let them get out to the cotton candy. *(Beat.)* Well, friends, as you can see, Cassidy Clarkson's horse, Starbright, is down and very quickly our world-class veterinary team is in the arena and will be doing whatever's needed for the horse. What a tough break, just seconds after clinching her first-ever Canadian title.

STARBRIGHT: Sunk dunk thump thump.

CASSIDY: Thump thump, Starry.

ANNOUNCER: Let's hope that Cassidy Clarkson of Claresholm isn't too wrecked from this. They raise them tough in the rodeo business, but there's nothing like your horse going down and staying down. We are so very sorry to have this happen to a very fine cowgirl and her horse, on the very last day of the Canadian Rodeo Championships.

Scene 5

CASSIDY is alone in the barn with her head down. The GODDESSES enter.

BB: Cassidy?

CASSIDY: Are you gonna tell me you told me so?

BB: No.

CASSIDY: That I shoulda known better?

JOYCE: No.

CASSIDY: Just say it, give me the gears. I know you want to.

JOYCE: It was an incredible ride.

EFFIE: You were a quiet rider, stayed in yer seat.

BB: And you let Starbright lead.

CASSIDY: What was I thinking?

JOYCE: You wanted to win.

CASSIDY: Yeah, I wanted to win too much.

Beat.

BB: Where is Starry?

CASSIDY: With the vet.

BB: What did the vet say?

CASSIDY: She'll never compete again.

I just thought, winning would solve... everything. That everything would be... That I wouldn't feel so lonely anymore, that I wouldn't feel so...lost or...That I could go home a winner. it would make everything feel okay again. But I made her fall because I didn't...I didn't put her first.

BB: You went down the wrong path—

CASSIDY: My Star—

BB: But it's not all your fault. We wanted to win just as much.

JOYCE: Maybe more.

CASSIDY: You only ever helped me.

BB: We wanted to help ourselves.

Beat.

There's something we gotta tell you.

BB looks at the other GODDESSES.

JOYCE: Go on.

EFFIE: Time's right.

Beat.

EFFIE: We're not who you think we are.

CASSIDY: You're not?

JOYCE: We're—

EFFIE: We're—

BB: We're...goddesses.

CASSIDY: Goddesses?

BB: Goddesses.

CASSIDY: Like, from heaven?

JOYCE: From a skybox.

Beat.

EFFIE: In the goddamn sky.

The GODDESSES are now glowing.

CASSIDY: Holy cow. You're—you're... How'd you do that?

EFFIE: Told ya, we're goddesses.

CASSIDY: You're...um, okay, yer like…magic cowgirls?

JOYCE: Goddess cowgirls.

CASSIDY: Goddess cowgirls…

EFFIE: We were the best of the best.

JOYCE: Shining stars with roaring fans.

BB: Hearts bound to our horses. We came down because we wanted—

JOYCE: Those crowds.

EFFIE: That rush.

BB: The wind. But it wasn't the right way.

JOYCE: We wanted to be who we once were.

EFFIE: We did it for us, but we should have done it for you.

BB: We're so sorry.

BB hugs CASSIDY.

EFFIE: BB's the real saint, of course…she's in it for the horses.

CASSIDY: I wouldn't have gotten this far without you.

EFFIE: No need to get sappy about it.

BB lets go of CASSIDY and goes to hug EFFIE who holds off.

EFFIE: Hold yer horses.

JOYCE: Take some time.

EFFIE: Have a breather, and when yer ready...

BB: Start looking for another horse,

JOYCE: Start preparing for the biggest outdoor rodeo.

CASSIDY: *(Beat.)* I'm not going.

EFFIE: But you earned yer spot.

BB: Starbright will understand.

JOYCE: Fans love you, know you.

CASSIDY: I'm not going to Calgary. I'm going home.

Scene 6

CASSIDY and STARRY in the field. CASSIDY pulls some apple out of her pocket.

CASSIDY: You okay?

STARBRIGHT: Yeaaaaaaah.

CASSIDY: Sweet sweet.

STARBRIGHT: Sweeeeet sweeet.

CASSIDY: Look at that stubble field, barn clean, chores done, open the barn door and stand in the sun.

STARBRIGHT: Hoooome.

CASSIDY: Home. *(Beat.)* This is where we belong, in the pasture—nothing better.

STARBRIGHT: Nuzzle nuzzle.

CASSIDY: Nuzzle nuzzle.

STARBRIGHT: Ruuuun.

CASSIDY: You wanna run the barrels?

STARBRIGHT: Yaaaaa!

CASSIDY: Okay, but just for fun, 'kay? We'll be easy on them, right, Star?

STARBRIGHT: Yeeahhhh eeassssy.

CASSIDY gets up on STARBRIGHT. The GODDESSES walk up.

JOYCE: Sit up, cowgirl, and face the sun. Show 'em your winning smile.

EFFIE: Stay wide on them turns.

BB: Don't tell Starbright what to do. Ask her.

CASSIDY: Gran was right, we have each other, and that's enough, more than enough.

Aaaand go!

The End.